I CAN READ ABOUT

ELEPHANTS

Written by C. J. Naden

Illustrated by Joel Snyder

Troll Associates

An elephant is not like any other animal. When you see one, you cannot mistake it for anything else.

Elephants are the second biggest animals in the world.

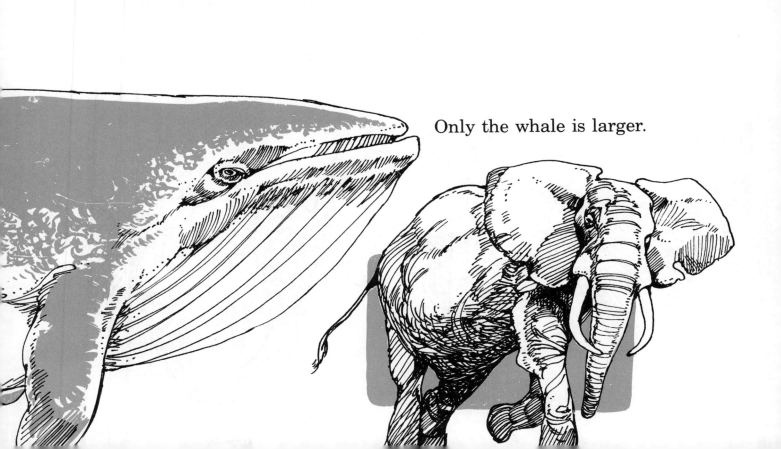

Only the whale is larger.

There are two kinds of elephants—African elephants and Asian elephants. It's easy to tell them apart. The African elephant has bigger ears. Their toes are different, too. The African elephant has four toenails on its front foot. The Asian elephant has five toenails.

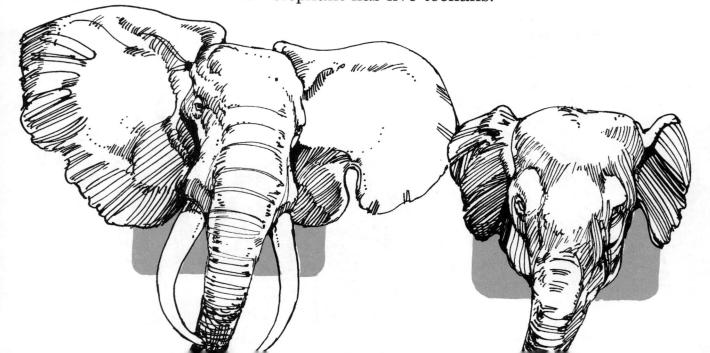

You can also tell the African elephant by its sloping forehead. The Asian elephant has a bulgy, rounded forehead.

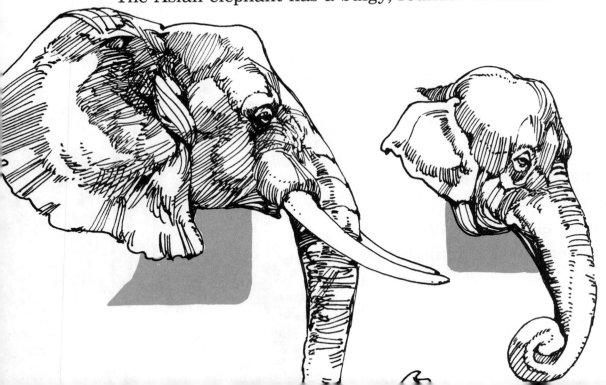

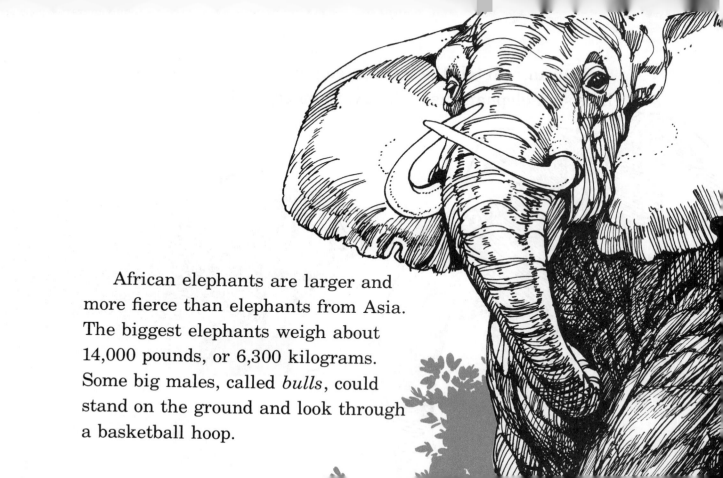

African elephants are larger and more fierce than elephants from Asia. The biggest elephants weigh about 14,000 pounds, or 6,300 kilograms. Some big males, called *bulls*, could stand on the ground and look through a basketball hoop.

Most elephants are gray. The African elephant is usually dark gray. The Asian elephant is usually light gray. But sometimes an *albino*, or white, elephant is born.

African elephants live
south of the Sahara Desert
in Africa.

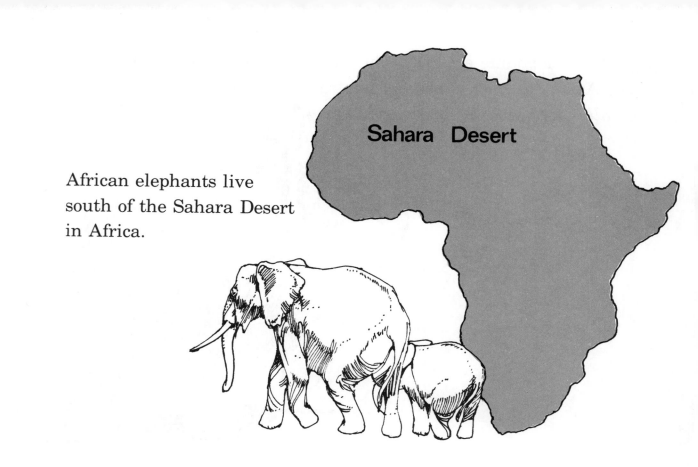

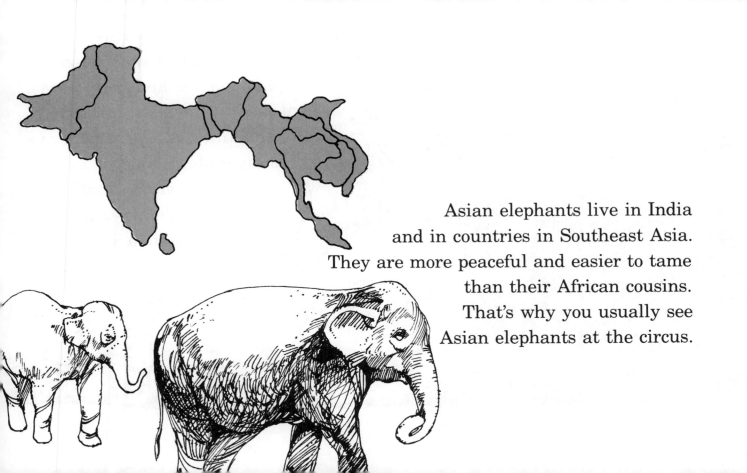

Asian elephants live in India
and in countries in Southeast Asia.
They are more peaceful and easier to tame
than their African cousins.
That's why you usually see
Asian elephants at the circus.

All elephants have leathery skin. Their skin is wrinkled and baggy-looking, like a suit that is too big. Elephants are called *pachyderms*. That means "having a thick skin." But this thick skin does not have a layer of fat under it to keep the animal warm. That's why elephants sometimes get stomachaches in cold weather.

On the sides of the
elephant's jaw are two
long ivory teeth. They
are called tusks. The elephant
uses its tusks to dig for food
and to fight when it is angry.

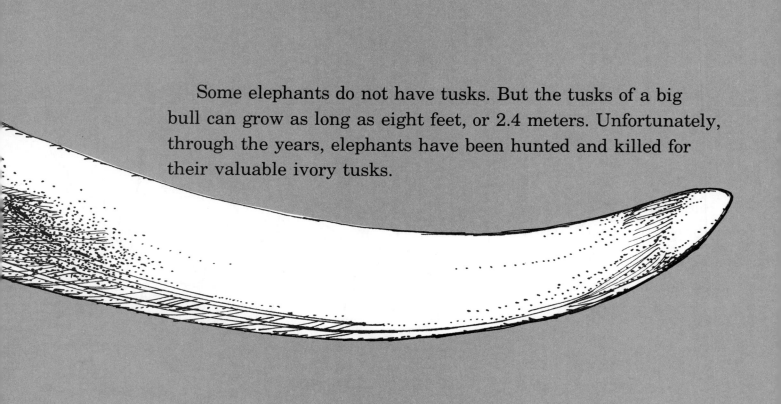

Some elephants do not have tusks. But the tusks of a big bull can grow as long as eight feet, or 2.4 meters. Unfortunately, through the years, elephants have been hunted and killed for their valuable ivory tusks.

The thing that really makes the elephant
different from all other animals is its amazing trunk.
The trunk is the elephant's nose
and hands. The elephant uses
its trunk for so many things
—to eat, to drink,
to carry logs, to fight,
to touch, and to smell.

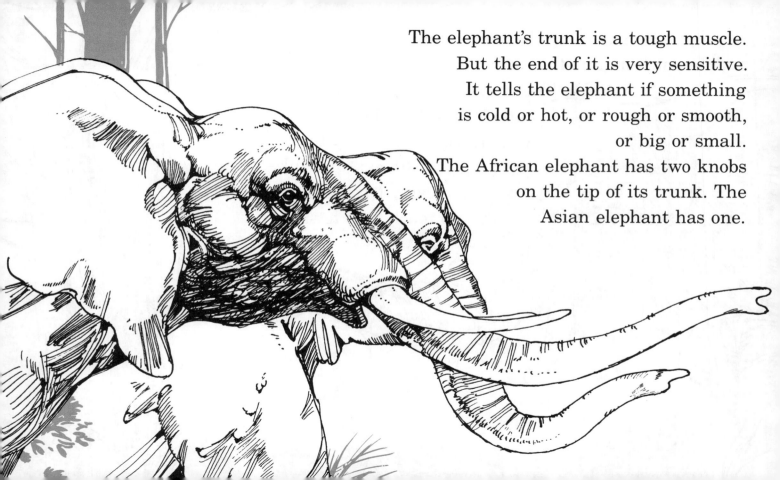

The elephant's trunk is a tough muscle.
But the end of it is very sensitive.
It tells the elephant if something
is cold or hot, or rough or smooth,
or big or small.
The African elephant has two knobs
on the tip of its trunk. The
Asian elephant has one.

Elephants stretch out their trunks to pat each other.

A mother elephant uses her
trunk to push her baby
in the right direction.

If an elephant feels that it is in danger, it raps its trunk sharply on the ground. This warns other elephants that something is wrong. A high and loud call means that the elephant is angry or in pain.

No other animal has a nose like
the elephant's nose. The elephant is always
sniffing, its trunk high in the air or poking along
the ground. Its sense of smell makes up for its
poor eyesight. The elephant hears well, but it
does not see well. It has tiny eyes and
long eyelashes.

Elephants love water. They are good swimmers even though they are so big. In the wild, elephants travel to water holes or rivers and wade in. They suck water into their long trunks, and then squirt it all over themselves. On a hot day, a shower feels very good. It also helps to keep the bugs away.

Elephants seem to be eating all the time. It takes
a lot of food to keep their huge bodies full.
In the wild, some big male elephants eat about five hundred
pounds, or 227 kilograms, of food every day.
They like all sorts of fruits and vegetables, and
leaves and bark.

The elephant reaches up with its trunk, grabs a tender
branch, and stuffs it into its mouth.

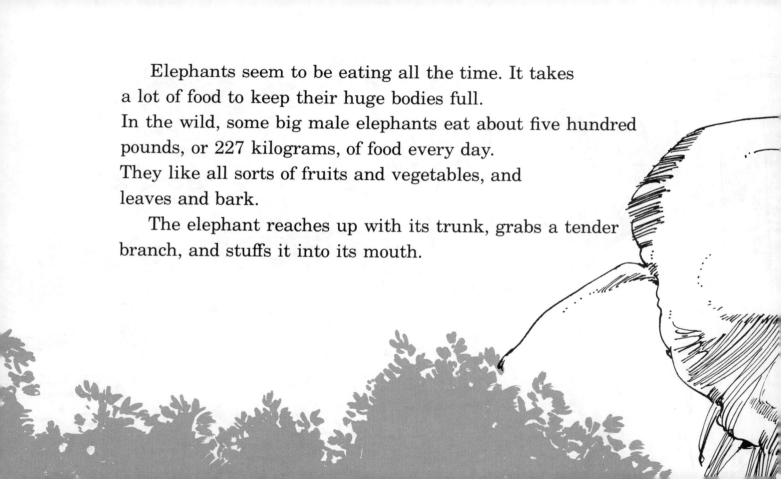

Because elephants are so large, they need room to hunt for food. Elephants do lots of damage as they hunt. The Asian elephant reaches up to break off tree branches. But the African elephant is more likely to knock over the whole tree.

In a circus or zoo, elephants might eat
150 pounds, or 68 kilograms, of hay each day,
along with a few bucketfuls of grain.
Elephants are very noisy eaters.
Their trunks gurgle, and their stomachs
grumble and growl.

You've heard the old saying, "An elephant never forgets." Maybe some elephants forget, but it really is true that they have good memories. Most elephants are very smart. Once they learn something, they usually remember it.

When an elephant is 20 years old, it is grown up.
In the wild, it may live more than 70 years.
A newborn elephant weighs about 200 pounds,
or 91 kilograms. A baby elephant is
called a *calf*.

The calf has tiny tusks. Its body is covered with fuzzy hair. As it grows up, the calf will grow long tusks and it will lose most of its hair.

An elephant usually has just one baby, but sometimes there are twins. It takes 22 months for a baby to be born, longer than any other animal. An hour or so after it is born, the little elephant can walk. The baby's mother takes good care of it. And there are usually a few "aunts" around to help, too.

Both African and Asian elephants live much the same way in the wild. They travel in herds, with 10 to 50 elephants in a herd. Usually they are led by an old and wise female, called a *cow*. As they walk through the jungle, elephants travel in a single file.

Elephants travel great distances in search of food and water.
They slowly shuffle through the jungle.
But any angry or frightened elephant
can reach a speed of 25 miles, or
40 kilometers, an hour
for a short time.

Elephants are usually quiet as they shuffle through the forest.
Yet they can make loud noises if they are afraid or angry.
Sometimes two bull elephants will get into a fight.
They try to hurt each other with their tusks.

Most of the time, elephants are peaceful. They get along well with other animals, perhaps because they are so big. However, very young elephants are sometimes hunted by hungry lions or tigers. If a baby is attacked, all the elephants in the herd will defend it.

Sometimes an old bull is driven away from the herd. He is often called a *rogue*. The rogue has a cranky disposition and is very dangerous. He may attack anyone on sight. Scientists say that the rogue's bad temper is often caused by a toothache!

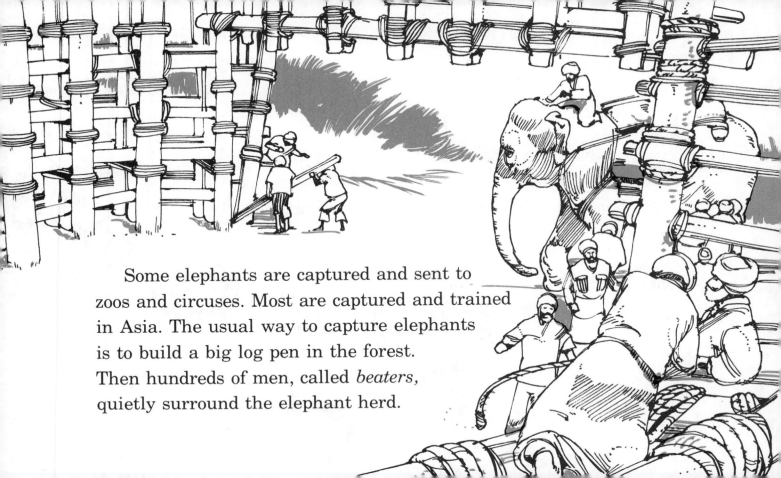

Some elephants are captured and sent to
zoos and circuses. Most are captured and trained
in Asia. The usual way to capture elephants
is to build a big log pen in the forest.
Then hundreds of men, called *beaters,*
quietly surround the elephant herd.

Now the beaters beat the bushes to make as much noise as they can. The elephants become frightened. The beaters drive them into the log pen.

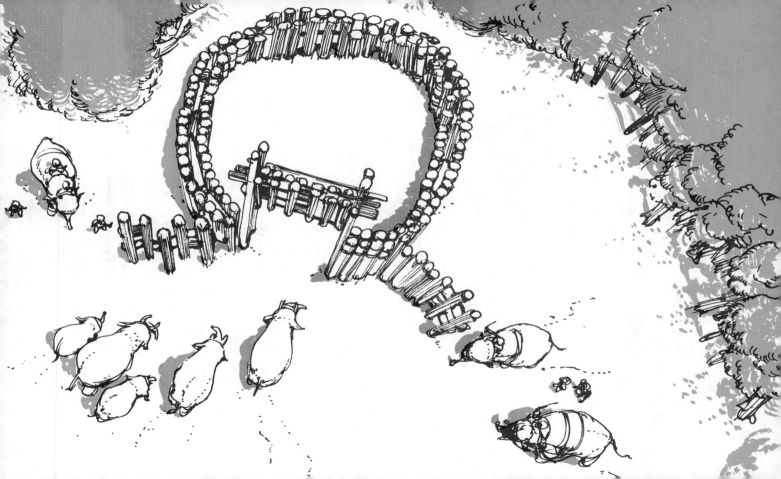

From early times, people have hunted elephants for ivory, or trained them for work. Elephants have been trained to carry lumber and heavy loads. Thousands of years ago, they were used in battle. Elephants went to war, carrying soldiers on their backs.

There is no other animal in the world today quite like the elephant. But it does have some relatives from the past. About forty million years ago, the first ancestor of the elephant appeared on earth. It did not have a trunk or tusk. It was about the size of a small pig. As time passed, the descendants of this animal grew trunks and tusks. They grew larger and larger.

Millions of years later, woolly mammoths and great mastodons appeared on earth. These big, shaggy relatives of the elephant were hunted by early people about ten thousand years ago. They, like other primitive animals, died out. All the mammoths and mastodons are gone now. Only the elephant lives on.

But how long will the elephant live? Elephants are in danger. There are not as many of them in the wild as there used to be. They have vanished entirely from some Asian countries. Part of the reason is their valuable ivory tusks. Although there are game laws to protect them, elephants are still killed.

In modern times, people are urged to "shoot" elephants with cameras, not guns. Countries in Africa and Asia have set aside land so that elephants and other animals can survive in the wild. Each year thousands of people visit these places.

With its trunk in the air and its ears flapping in the breeze, the great elephant is an amazing sight. In all the world, there is no other animal like it.